Follow
Your Passion

Attain Peace, Happiness and Financial Security by Doing What You Love

K. ELIZABETH

©2016

Introduction

Do you find your job emotionally draining?
Are you sick of being stuck in a rut?
Is it your dream to break free of the rat race?

If you answered "yes" to any of these questions then this book is for you!

I myself spent a large chunk of my life working in the corporate sector. Each day was a battle between what I wanted and the figures on my bank statement. It was mentally exhausting and emotionally draining.

Until one day I simple decided that enough was enough. I couldn't spend the best part of my life working 9 to 5 at a desk for a cause that I did not even care for. It was then that I decided to return to my lifelong passion of writing.

Ever since I made that decision, life has been sweeter and much more happier.

My experience made me realize that there are so many people out there who are stuck in a similar situations. They want to leave their jobs to find and follow their true life passions but are unable to do so because of numerous reasons.

Hence this book was written to help out all those people who need a little push and a little reassurance to break free from their mundane routines.

This book includes motivational but real talk, helpful insights and lots of anecdotes to make you feel like a part of the journey. The book was written to encourage you and support you-like a good friend!

Continue reading to find and follow your passion so that you can lead a life of your dreams!

Table of Contents

This document is geared towards providing exact and reliable information in regards to the topic and issue covered. The publication is sold with the idea that the publisher is not required to render accounting, officially permitted, or otherwise, qualified services. If advice is necessary, legal or professional, a practiced individual in the profession should be ordered.

From a Declaration of Principles which was accepted and approved equally by a Committee of the American Bar Association and a Committee of Publishers and Associations.

In no way is it legal to reproduce, duplicate, or transmit any part of this document in either electronic means or in printed format. Recording of this publication is strictly prohibited and any storage of this document is not allowed unless with written permission from the publisher. All rights reserved.

The information provided herein is stated to be truthful and consistent, in that any liability, in terms of inattention or otherwise, by any usage or abuse of

The Curse of Over Thinking

A Thinking Man by Wesley Nitsckie

It is often touted that little children are the epitome of everything that a man should aspire to be. They are happy, mostly content with what they have, free of societal bounds and pure of heart. A little child doesn't have a toy? No problem! He will pick up a stick from the ground and pretend that it's a sword. Even if there is no stick, he will run around making funny noises and will think that he is riding a motorbike. Their imagination knows no bounds. Similarly their happiness knows no bounds either.

Remember your own time as a kid. You might have some scattered memories here and there. Some happy, like getting your favorite chocolate and some sad like the death of an old pet but what is the thing that is common in all these memories? What is the thing that is common in all children?

I will give you a moment to think about it.

You would have come up with some very valid points but in my opinion, the thing that is common in all children is that they do not think. Now this may come across as not a very nice thing to say but I mean it in a very genius way.

When a child does something, he doesn't think about the impact it is going to have. Even if it is something stupid like picking up some candy without asking. A child does it because he simply feels like doing it. He doesn't ask his "heart" about what it feels about the candy. He just does it. Action is closely followed by desire. There are no other factors in count. Not even the fear of consequences.

Now fast forward to adult life.
What do we, as adults do?
We over think every single thing! Don't believe me?

Just imagine that you have a plate of potato chips in front of you. Your heart is tempted by the crispy goodness. Your mouth is watering but then you are reminded that you need to fit into that little black dress for whatever event. So you fight a mental battle between the delight of potato chips and the praise of a slim figure. You treat it almost as a mathematical question.

Now what would a child do?
He would just simply grab a fistful and shove it in his mouth because he freaking wants to!

This is the kind of courage that we as adults lack. We lose the simplicity of action to the complexity of thought. We are never in the moment and we are always thinking about the consequences of this and the effects of that.

This naturally extends to our career life as well. So many of us just want to do things, even like to do things, our heart screams for it yet every single day, we fight a mental battle between the action we want to take and the action that we are "supposed" to take.

In my book, there is no such thing as something that you are "supposed" to do. This "supposed" concept is a result of over thinking. You cannot exercise your passion until you get rid of this over thinking.

I remember a movie that I saw. It was titled "Yes Man". You might have seen it as well. It revolved around a man who resolves to say "yes" to everything that comes his way for a certain period of time. This practice brought about some very pleasant and unexpected changes to his life.
Nevertheless, the moral of the story was that sometimes weighing things too much can be a curse and you should just "do".

I would suggest that before we start on the journey of finding your passion, you try to be a yes man/woman as well. Even if it is for a short period of time like three days or so. You might be pleasantly surprised by the way it turns around your life even in the little ways. This would enable you to jumpstart your way into finding and conquering your passion!

You Have What You Need

By Ota Photos

The pursuit of happiness" is the lamest phrase to have ever been said. How are you supposed to pursue happiness? What are you doing when you are not pursuing happiness? Are you pursuing sadness then? The concept is utterly idiotic because happiness is something that you don't need to pursue. As clichéd as it might sound, it is something that comes to you when you open yourself to all sorts of opportunities.

Now here's the scary part. Opening up to the opportunities is something that is all roses and jasmines as long as these are opportunities like a job promotion or trying out a new dish but things get scary and uncertain when these opportunities are disguised as a low paying job or brand new proposals in another states/countries.

Why do we refuse such opportunities?
Or a better question would be, why do we refuse to create these opportunities for ourselves?

The answer is that it is because we have created a false sense of security around us. We like to think that if we have a good credit account then we are supposedly safe from whatever life decides to throw at us.
But do all people who have a lot of money saved up pull through in life? By that logic, no celebrity should ever commit suicide. No rich person should ever die in a tsunami.

This false sense of security is not just limited to finances. Our emotional connections also give us a false sense of security. Why do people keep on hanging to abusive relationships? Why do fighting couples who have no hope for redemption file for divorce so late?

The answer is simple!
Familiarity provides a sense of security. We think that

all the things we have, or the things we are supposed to have (materialistically or emotionally), we actually need them.

We think we need Netflix, the internet, the DSLR camera, the huge penthouse, a functioning car, a doting partner, fat grandchildren etc.

The truth is that you don't need any of these. Within yourself, you already have all that you need. Pursuing these does not equate to pursuing happiness but we mistakenly think that the two are equivalent.

You might be thinking that what does Netflix or fat grandchildren have to do with finding your passion?

Well it has everything to do with it because these are the things that hold you back from exercising your passion. 99% of the time, it is something that you think you need that holds you back from living the life you want to live.

Right now, get a pen and paper. This book can wait while you go and fetch them.

Now that you have some writing equipment, list down all the things that you think you "need". Don't be biased. Just list all the things that you think you cannot survive without (food, shelter and air not included). You can even list random things you love like potato chips (I love potato chips, can you tell?) or watching movies with your boy/girlfriend.

Done?

Now put this away. We'll come back to the list at the end.

What Do You Want To Do With Your Life?

A Cowboy Needs a Porpoise in Life by Alan Levine

The term "Life Purpose" is borderline scary. Motivational movies of rags to riches stories have drilled it into our minds that you need to devote your entire life towards one specific thing. That if we are not like Steve Jobs, living and breathing our work, we are a failure in our lives.

This thinking had led us into believing that we, as humans are one dimensional beings who should devote their entire life to doing one singular task and never think about anything else. This is easier said than done.

Humans are multi-dimensional. At one point, we can like a lot of things. I will quote myself as an example. I am someone who loves to read and write. I have always loved to read. It is my escape, it is my survival mechanism but I am also someone who really loves makeup and all things beauty.

Stereotypical images have taught us that both cannot co-exist. That if you love reading and are a geek at heart, you can't also be the popular person of the school. In truth, there can be many grey areas to a person.

Some people are fortunate enough to know their passion in life from the start. There are kids who just know what they want to be. They know that they want to paint. They know that they want to sing. They know that they want to build motors. Some people just know that and are willing to work towards it but most of us are not as clear.

Between the ages of 18 and 25, people usually change their aspirations faster than you can say "life goals".

One minute you want to be a singer, the next minute you want to be an accountant. This is very common.

Then what is your life passion?

There is no straightforward answer to this question and trust me, nobody, not even a life coach can answer this question for you. As a person, you enjoy many things in life. Many things catch your fancy but true, lasting, career oriented success can only come if you are willing to combine that passion of choice with hard work and determination.

Nobody can solve it for you but here is a set of questions that you can answer to figure it out for yourself.

> What is it about yourself as a child that you miss the most?

This does not include memories associated with others. Something that you had and now you think that you have lost it or it is long gone. Aspiring writers often start writing at a very early age. At least this was very true for me. I would write absurd stories or even attempt poetry. To be honest, the poetry was very bad but I still continued because at that time, I was doing it for myself.

As we grow up, the fear of reactions takes over us. We begin thinking that we must do things in such a way that they please people. People like me, stop writing because they are afraid of the reaction that it will bring.

Is there something from your childhood that you miss? Something that you loved to do but gave up because unconsciously you were seeking approval from other people.

What are you horrible at?

Nobody is ever good at everything. If you are good in math, there is a chance that you are not so good with languages.

When we used to do MCQs in school, one method that we employed to get the correct answer was to first cross out the obviously wrong answers.

This is the same concept. For you to figure out what you are really good at, you must first eliminate all the options at which you are horrible. Whatever it is, write it down honestly.

Nobody knows your weaknesses better than you.

What can make you forget food?

Maybe I am a little biased on this because I am a hard core foodie but anyway, food is a basic necessity and at some level, all of us desire it. Some people more than others.

Apart from a new crush, is there anything you do that can even make you forget even food? That when you are doing it, you can even forget to eat for hours at a stretch.

What do you want to be remembered by?

We are all going to die one day. It is an inevitable fact.

In most cases, people die and then a few people mourn and then everyone moves on but in some rare cases, a death shakes the entire world or an entire nation. For example, like the death of John Kennedy.

When you die, what do you want to be remembered as? How do you want people to remember you?

Some people want people to remember them as being nice, kind and helpful. Others want to be remembered as being leaders and game changers. Which one are you? And what kind of game changer?

Figure out your order of priorities

Everyone has a set of priorities. Nobody is ever too busy for anything.
Now that you know what your childhood aspiration or hidden talent was, you need to figure out where it stands in your life.

Let's assume that it is music. Now are you willing to sacrifice all other activities for the sake of music? Can you commit to a life involving music for up to 10 hours a day?

If excuses like "..but I like watching Netflix more than I enjoy practicing on the guitar" are popping up in your head then forget it. This is not your one true aspiration.

However, if your excuses involve fear of reaction then it is another matter altogether and will be discussed later.

Can you face embarrassment for it?

Once you have figured out your set of priorities, the most important question lingers on.

What is it that you can even face critique and embarrassment for? No matter how good you are, there will be a time when you will fail and somebody will not like what you do. Are you willing to put up your brave face and take it up without losing sight of your initial goal?

If yes, then kudos to you! That's the true mark of passion!

You don't have to answer all these questions in one seating. Sit down, focus, contemplate and take your time. You can even answer them over a period of few days. There is no need to rush.

By the time, you are honestly done answering, you would have singular option shining like a beacon. You would have figured it out but it wouldn't come as a surprise to you because you knew it in your heart all along.

The Importance of Taking Action

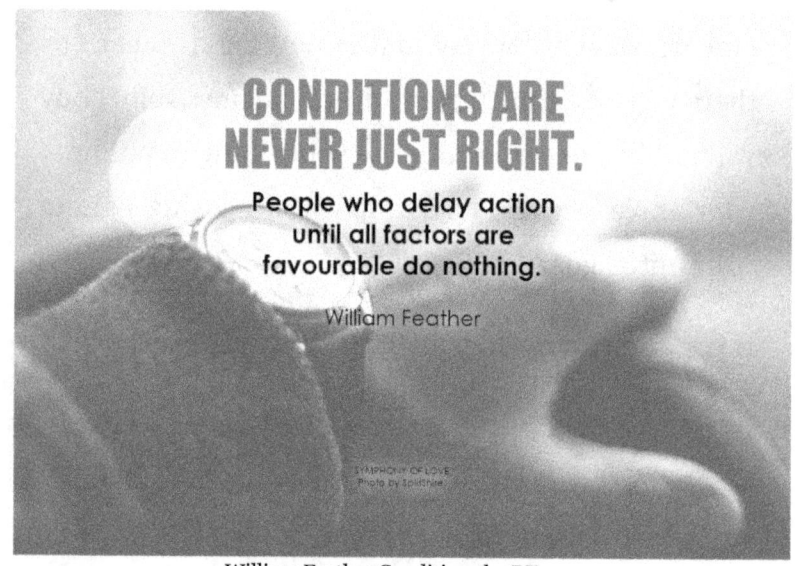

CONDITIONS ARE NEVER JUST RIGHT.

People who delay action until all factors are favourable do nothing.

William Feather

William Feather Conditions by BK

At some deep level, like a child, we all know what we want to do. However, as we discussed earlier, our curse of over thinking prevents us from actually doing anything about it.

A common misconception that exists is that you can only take action when you are feeling inspired enough to actually change things. To some extent it might be true. Like it is said for smokers that they can only quit if they themselves want it. Nobody else can force them to quit.

It is all fairly true but here is a catch. Motivation and action are very much interrelated. Both of these are interdependent on each other. Mere mental motivation without any action is useless. It is like that uncle who keeps on saying that he can quit smoking but he never actually does it.

Similarly, if you want to turn your life around to follow you passion then you need to act. Irrespective of motivation.

But how can you act without being inspired?
You might ask.

Well in my opinion you can!

Remember the time when you were a young kid and you had to prepare your exam. Nobody ever feels inspired to actually cram for exams but once you start doing it, you get into the flow. Like when you do math questions, the first few problems are always the hardest and then you kind of get the hang of it and it becomes easier. As they become easier, you are motivated to practice more.

Life is like that series of math problems. Unless you begin, unless you solve one, you will never get the hang of it.

So no matter how uninspired or doubtful you are about your goal, about your passion-just start with it! Don't waste time planning for years ahead and saving money. Just jump in. Even in a small way, start today! Or better start right now but do take some action.

I am not suggesting that give up your job and family and all other things to focus on your passion. You'll tire yourself out that way and it will be an open invitation for problems but take some time out of your day for now. An hour or even half an hour and devote it to your passion.

Do not let it remain a thing of your mind. Convert it into a physical entity. When I thought that I wanted to write, initially I just thought about it. I would dream about how I would write about this and write about that but soon enough I realized that this was no good. There is no dream unless you take action so I began keeping a daily journal. I propelled myself into taking action according to my dream and so should you!

It doesn't matter what your passion is. If you want to have a restaurant, start studying about them. Get some books, visit some ventures, talk to some owners but do something!

If you want to be an engineer, start tinkering with the objects of your desire. Watch YouTube videos, visit mechanic shops but do something that propels you in that direction.

Taking action will also tell you if your desire for your passion is strong enough. If it is your one true passion, you'll be motivated by the action and not tired by it. If dreaming was easy and you are not inspired by the actual action, then this might not be it.

True and lasting success always comes from action. It all starts with dreaming but it should always result in action. From all the success stories that I've read (true to fact stories and not clichéd underdog movies), the common factor that I have deduced is that success is more reliant on action backed by talent rather than sheer talent alone. A doer will always defeat a dreamer. There cannot be any success without action. Period.

Doubts, Procrastination and Second Thoughts

Dec.9 By Bhumi Finding Herself

Being doubtful of ourselves is a part of being human. Every single day, every moment, we are doubtful of what we are going to do. We are afraid of the results and the consequences. We are more worried about the destination than the actual journey. This is the curse of over thinking.

However, saying that one should just stop thinking such thoughts would be an over simplification. The more you tell yourself to not think about penguins, the more you will think about penguins. That is just how human brain works.

I am going to go off the bat now and say that doubts and fears never suffocated a passion, procrastination and refusal to take action did.

Having fears is natural and it's okay and you should embrace it. It is okay to feel afraid if you are leaving your job to feed your passion. It is okay to worry about the future of your children and the well being of your family. What is not okay is using that fear as an excuse to procrastinate.

Instead use your fear to propel you. The fear of failure. The fear of living a life of mediocrity and unhappiness-where you wake up every day to go to a job you don't like. To spend your weeks waiting for Sundays. That kind of life is fearful. Use that fear of inadequacy to push yourself. Fear can be your ally.

You do not have to take a massive leap of faith right in the beginning. No sane person would advise you to leave everything and blow off all your savings to play drums all day long. No, you need to start slow but you need to start to establish your footing.

Our real enemy here is our tendency to procrastinate. The long "breaks", the constant delays and the "tomorrow" mentality. Whatever passion you have, set time aside for it in your day. Make it your priority. If you are not making it your priority, then it is your fault. Not anybody else's.

Often we mistake procrastination for "planning". Making mental notes about how we will do this and how we will do that. Some of us even have elaborate mental plans of what we want to do in the next ten years. Plan reasonable but do not allow your life to engulfed by them. Do not live your life by the line. Instead, jump straight in. Unless you are ready to begin, to face what life throws at you and to take it head on, you can't really do anything. Stop planning and start doing!

Let me tell you a secret.
Every job is horrible at some point!

Yes, you read it right. You might hate your current job but there is no such promise that you will love every second of your passion job. Even jobs that are considered "dream jobs" can be pretty crappy at some times.

For example, renowned makeup artist Jordan Liberty says that 60% of the job does not require any creativity at all. It is about proper sanitation, working under pressure and keeping your clients happy even at the sake of your own vision but you need to power through because at the end of the day you are doing it for the freedom of creativity it gives you. That freedom might not be every day but it is there. Even Pat McGrath (another celebrated makeup artist) does not create creative, avant-garde looks in every sitting. You have to bear the not-so-good parts for the sake of the great options that your passion offers.

Expecting that your dream job would be all rainbows and unicorns is absurd and stupid. Every job has its own set of struggles. Even the dream jobs. Your passion job will have its own sets of struggles as well. You will only know about them when you will start to work the job.

Part of lasting success is to understand this as a life fact and come to peace with it. Every job requires struggle and at some point you will hate your job, no matter how much you wanted it.

Think of it like a relationship. You are dating someone who is the vision of your dreams. You are so much in love and are committed/married. No matter how much head over heels in love you are, there will be fights, disagreements and shouting. There will even be times when you will hate each other but do you want to leave? Of course not!

Same in the case with your life passion. There will be times when you will be tired of it but that is okay because at the end of the day, it is still what you genuinely want.

Just like relationships need work and a little TLC, your passion needs these two things as well. It will not all miraculously set into place. You will need hard work, determination and an unflinching attitude to get where you want to get.

Want to hear another secret?

Sometimes even Brad Pitt hates his job.

That should make you feel better.

Let's Talk Finances

Numbers, Money, Calculating, Calculations by Pexels

Nearly every self-help, motivational book starts with the question, "If money was out of question, would you still do the job that you're doing?"
The honest answer for most people is "no" but this is a hypothetical question. Money is never out of question. At least not in this world.

Money is our lifeline. Without money, there is no food, there is no clothing, there is no shelter and there is no list of things that we made earlier. Hence the idea of opting for something that will generate very little money is understandably scary.

The question is not about whether we need money or not. Of course we do need money but it is about how much money do we need. How much of it is ever enough?

If you know the average capitalist mind, then money is never enough.

So how do you decide how much money do you even need?

Well nobody can figure it out for you but yourself. We made the list of things you love and we also made a priority list earlier in the book. It is your task to decide where your passion stands in the list of the things you love. Is it above them or is it below them? That will give you the answer of how much money you need.

Say, your passion is singing. I cannot promise you that one day you will wake up and you will become as successful as Adam Levine or you will start making the kind of money he makes. Nobody can promise you that but what I can indeed promise you is that if you keep marching on, do not procrastinate and pursue your passion honestly, you will have enough money to lead a reasonable life and above all, you will have peace of heart.

If that is something you are not keeping in mind or it is something that you are not willing to settle for, then please reconsider your priorities. What is it that you want? Do you want to sing or do you want to sing for a large audience?

There is a difference between the two. The first one is about you. You are singing because it brings you happiness of the heart. The second one is about people. You want to sing because you desire the fame it brings. Wanting recognition and appreciation is different from blindly desiring fame.

Following your passion and desiring fame are two very different things.

Sometimes these two end up being one but at the core, there are just very, very different.

If the sole reason you want to follow your passion is to become rich and famous, then it is not about your passion but about the later two. You just want to become rich and famous, no matter how.

Again, the question of how much money comes into light. Most people are able to make a decent living by simply following their passion but not all go on to become Lionel Messi. The professional aspect of your passion is very different from the core of your passion. Trust me on that.

Take me for example, I make a reasonable, comfortable living by doing what I have always loved to do - writing but am I living the lifestyle of Paris Hilton? Of course not! But am I content? Yes!

I sincerely wish that you become the star of whatever passion you decide to follow but how much money do you need to generate to make it actually worthwhile is something that you, yourself need to decide.

Having It All

Alone/Together by Ian Mottoo

In the past six or seven decades, the world has changed drastically. People are more connected, life is seemingly easier and within a click you can be anywhere in the world (at least virtually). It has also made us more restless, more ambitious and more vicious in a sense.

Back in the day, the son of a baker grew up to be a baker. That was how life worked. Businesses ran in families and people committed themselves to whatever job their family had held. Whether it was good or bad, is another debate altogether.

Then came the concept of the "land of opportunity".
America. The Big Apple. Places where you could
transform yourself into anyone you want. It didn't
matter where you came from. As long as you had the
drive, you could achieve anything. The American
Dream.

What is the quintessential essence of it?
What this concept did was that it multiplied the
opportunities available to every single one of us.
Previously, the son of a baker could only be a baker.
That was the only opportunity available to him but
now, the opportunities are endless.

This is obviously a good thing in the sense that it has
allowed people to expand their horizons. The son of a
baker would not necessarily be a good cook because
that is not how genetics work. Now, if he is not good
at cooking, he has the opportunity to explore other
options.

However, like everything there is a but.. It is that the
more opportunities we have, the more opportunities
we are inadvertently missing out on. For example,
back in the day most women stayed at home to cook,
clean and take care of the children. Very few had other

options. Now-a-days, it is very different. All sorts of career opportunities are now open to women, which is amazing but it also means that somewhere somehow something will be missed.

You can be a career oriented, top of the rung CEO but you also want to be a full time doting mom who is present to witness every single moment of your children's life.
Unfortunately, you cannot have both. Unless some kind of technology is developed that allows us to be in two places at one time, this seems like a impossible dream.

Yet so many of us want both.

We want to be famous, yet we want private time. We want to eat as we please but we also want to be super skinny.
Unfortunately, this is not how life works.

When people start following their passion or decide to follow their passion, they hold back because they are afraid of missing out on the mediocrity of their lives. They want to excel yet they want to remain in their known, comfortable life.

Success never comes from comfort zones.

Even after you've had success or what you consider to be success, there is always something that is going to be missed out. That is just how life is. You are either going to watch the beautiful sunset or attend that party. You can't have both.

The sooner you come to terms with this basic fact of life, the better it would be.

But why talk about it here?
Because when people want to take the initiative of following their passion, it is not just about what they want to do. It is also about what they will not be doing. For you to be dedicating yourself to drumming, you would have to miss out on office lunches and Christmas parties and the social life associated with a traditional 9 to 5 job.

Making any change requires sacrifice. Sacrifice of all the opportunities that you would be missing. So at the end of the day, it is a choice. A choice between the opportunities you have now and the opportunities you will have if you make the switch. No matter what, one of these will be missed out.

Following your passion is no different. You won't ever be able to have it all. Such a thing doesn't exist.

Though, if it is your one true passion, it should not stop you because following your dream would have all the opportunities you've ever truly wanted.

Differentiating Positive and Negative Feedback

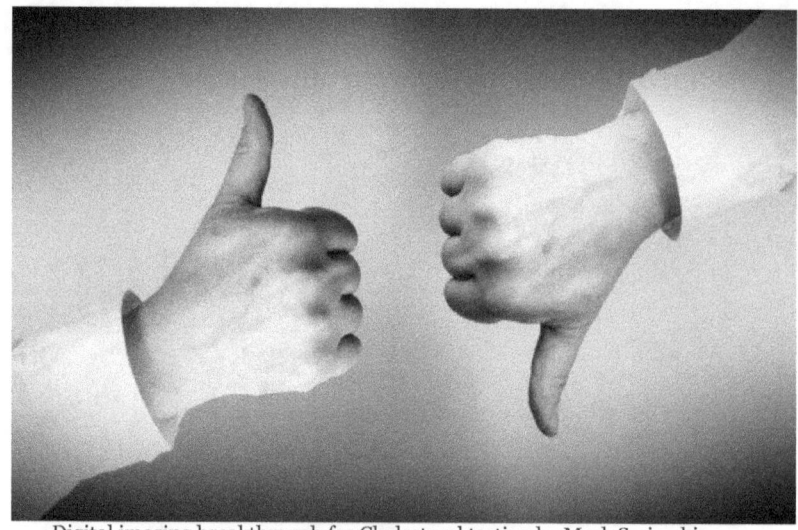

Digital imaging breakthrough for Cholesterol testing by Mark Scrimshire

There's this very famous quote by Dita Von Tease, "You can be the ripest, juiciest peach and there's still going to be somebody who hates peaches"

I would go as far as to say that truer words haven't been spoken. When we were talking about finding your passion, I mentioned how you must be ready to face embarrassment and critique for whatever line you are choosing. People will criticize you-always! No matter how good you are, there will be someone who doesn't like your work.

Though a common misconception that is present in a lot of dreamers is that they mistake all kind of critique as the one that is intended to pull them down. The mentality that, "Oh you're criticizing me because you don't want me to succeed" is very common amongst aspiring people.

In some cases, it might be true but it is definitely not the case in all scenarios. Sometimes you might be getting heat for a genuine reason. Improvement is a constant part of life. There can be no life without evolution and improvement. A stagnant life is a dead life.

Similar is the case with your passion. You can have a dream of being the president of the United States. It is a legit dream, as long as you are willing to work for it. Some people might laugh at you while others might encourage you. Some may even say that your chances are low because you are not a good public speaker. This critique may sound harsh but it could be true.

Being a good orator is a huge part of being a successful politician. You might have great ideas about the development of the country but unless you can convey them correctly, your chances are less.

So instead of getting defensive about every critique and labeling it as "hate", "jealousy" and "malice", try to look at it with an objective eye. Maybe there is some hidden gem of truth in that. Maybe you could use it to help your case. To work on yourself and better yourself.

There is a very fine line between positive and negative feedback. Not all positive feedback comes sugar coated but it could still be helpful to you, only if you choose to listen.

It is very important to not let the irrational hate bring you down but it is just as important to keep your mind open about suggestions, improvements and possible opportunities.

Looking For a Market

Presentation Training by Geralt

This book focuses on making a career out of your passion and not just keeping it as a side hobby. For any work to be made a career, you need a market. According to the laws of Economics, there is always a market for everything, you just have to find it. It is a simple rule of supply and demand.

If you are at the right place, at the right time, you can fill in the supply and demand gap and hence reap success. The trick is to keep looking. Have a sharp eye and see how a situation can benefit you and your passion.

For example, I once read this story of a man on Humans of New York who was a professional dog walker. Now that's an unconventional profession. That man said that he loved dogs. He was a tough looking guy who hated the previous jobs he had held. He looked around and saw that so many people didn't get the time to walk their dogs even though it was a need. So he put on some tough gear and went door to door to offer his services. Eventually someone agreed and his first session began. The man was naturally good with dogs and he looked tough like a soldier, so it gave the image that he knew what he was doing and could manage a pack of dogs. So it began. Now that man has a company of dog walkers, all dressed like him.

What that man did was that he analyzed his strengths and went on to find a market according to them. He focused on what he wanted and what he could give and he found a job that he loved doing. This is something that you need to do as well.

Just a little spark of creativity, ability to think out of the box and a willingness to take risks will open vast markets for you and your work. Here are a few pointers to help you along the way;

Intern/Assistant

Look for someone in your field of choice who is looking for an intern or an assistant. It doesn't have to be some big firm. Even a single person actually working in that field would do. It will give you an idea about the actual work setup of your field.

Lower Prices

There is always some demand for cheaper work. Even though it is not something that you want to keep doing for long term, it is still good to have some work experience under your belt. Start offering your services to NGO's, friends and even colleagues.

For example, if your passion is to be a public speaker, you can volunteer to coach a school debate team. This will keep you in touch with your work and will give you the action push that you need and who knows? Opportunities may stem from there.

However one thing to keep in mind is that do not keep on doing underpaid work. It can be an energy sucker and eventually you will have a herd of people who will be willing to milk you for very little in return. As your repute builds and experience increases, so should your rates.

Build a Portfolio

This is not applicable for every field but if your passion involves content creation then build a portfolio. Have a hard copy and a website that displays it all so that people can easily come across it. When people can see your work easily, they are more likely to approach you.

Promote Shamelessly

You are your own product. Market and promote yourself. Spread the word in your area and amongst family/friends. Ask them to refer you and tell other people as well. If you have a successful job, ask your employers to refer you to other people as well. There is nothing to be ashamed or embarrassed about. Are soft drinks brands embarrassed that they shamelessly promote their drinks everywhere? No! And neither should you.

Think outside the box

Great success comes from understanding the demand of the market and then coming forward to fill it. I cannot suggest anything certain for it because it would be specific to your situations but look around you and listen. What are people complaining about? What do they want? What do you want? Is there something that is needed that isn't available? A lot of great services/products were born from the fact that the creators were themselves unsatisfied with the available options. Pay attention and then act in line of that.

Conclusion

Thank you for reading this book.

I hope that you found it of help.

When I decided to write this book, my aim was to help people realize that they had it in them to be successful at whatever they desired. I know the pain of working in corporate sector. How painful and often fruitless it is. So I wanted to offer help to other people based on my personal experiences.

The next step is to answer the questions honestly, make a list and jump right in. Do not plan too much but take action because ultimately it is action that leads you to success.

Thank you!

K. Elizabeth

www.ingramcontent.com/pod-product-compliance
Lightning Source LLC
Chambersburg PA
CBHW070413190526
45169CB00003B/1244